How Music Works

By Donald Kalbach
and Joyce Kalbach

CELEBRATION PRESS
Pearson Learning Group

Contents

Music All Around Us

Music is all around us. We hear music from the radio and on television. We hear music in stores and in concert halls. We even hear it in elevators. Music follows us everywhere.

What is music? A dictionary might say that music is organized sound. That's not the whole story, though. The sound of a train on its tracks is organized, too. Is it music? The sound of a person walking is organized. Is that music?

Music is everywhere in our lives.

Music is more than just organized sound. It is an art and a science. It is based on mathematical ideas. For instance, when you read music in order to sing or play it, you count beats. People in some cultures mostly use the voice to make music. They may add **percussion** sounds, such as stamping their feet while singing. They might hit something with a stick. Some music uses just instruments. Other music uses voices and instruments. While music takes many forms, it has certain things in common. It shows feelings. It is made up of many ideas.

drumming with a bamboo log

A symphony orchestra creates music with many different instruments.

A mariachi (mar ee AH chee) band in Mexico is made up mostly of stringed instruments.

You will discover some of those ideas in this book. Different cultures have their own music. Music is a big part of what makes a culture unique.

Music has many different uses within each culture. It can make you want to dance. It can make you feel proud of your country. It can be used to help a person sleep. It may be used for entertainment.

People from different cultures often share their music with others. This helps people to learn about each other.

How Music Is Written

When you read letters of the alphabet, you are reading a code. When you read the letter *b* aloud, for example, you make a certain sound.

Written music is also a code. Imagine seeing a note on a music **staff**, the horizontal lines on a sheet of music. When you read the note, you make a certain sound, or **tone**. The note tells you whether to make the tone a high or a low **pitch**. The note also tells how long the tone must last. That length of time is called a **duration**.

The key signature tells us how many **sharps** or **flats** there are in the music.

The clef sign here tells us that the second line (counting from the bottom) is G.

The **time signature** is not a fraction, but it is read like one. Here, it says, "There are four quarter notes (or notes that add up to four quarters) in every measure."

In one way, reading music is easier than reading words. For example, the letter *a* has different sounds. It might sound like the *a* in *bake*, the *a* in *back*, or the *a* in *talk*. In music, a written note on a staff always has the same pitch and duration. It doesn't matter how often the note is played or sung.

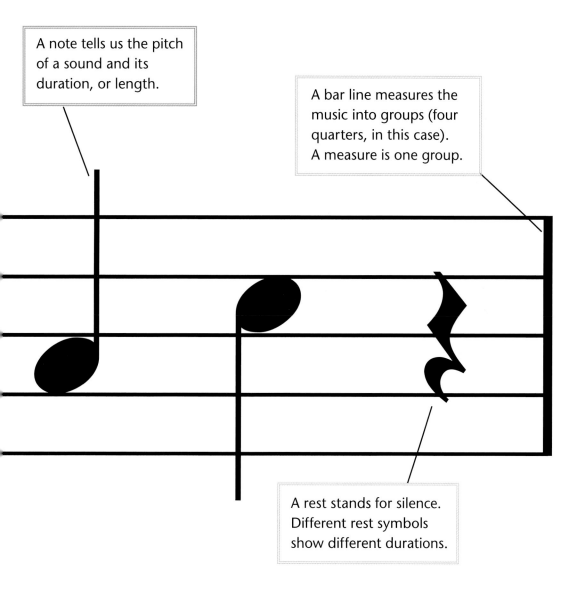

A note tells us the pitch of a sound and its duration, or length.

A bar line measures the music into groups (four quarters, in this case). A measure is one group.

A rest stands for silence. Different rest symbols show different durations.

Rhythm

Rhythm is the way notes are measured. It tells us the pattern of long or short notes.

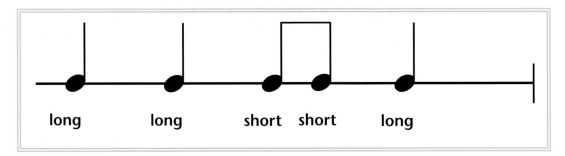

| long | long | short | short | long |

In a rhythm pattern, each note may have the same or a different duration. Percussion instruments are often used to play rhythm patterns, or to keep the beat in music.

To show the kinds of long and short notes in musical rhythm, you can use the example of a pie. A whole pie is like a whole note. A pie divided in half is like two half notes. The duration of each half note is half the time of a whole note. A pie divided into quarters, or fourths, is like four quarter notes. Divide those quarter notes in half, and you get eighth notes.

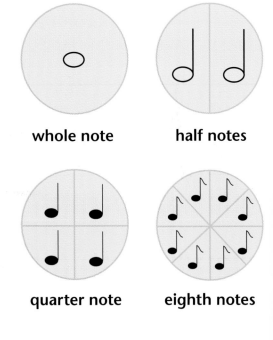

whole note   half notes

quarter note   eighth notes

How much faster than a whole note would an eighth note be played?

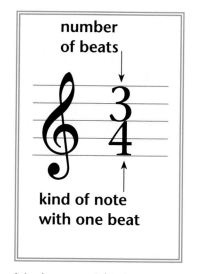

number
of beats

3
4

kind of note
with one beat

Music set at 3/4 time means there are three quarter-note beats per measure.

The rhythm of a piece of music is shown in the time signature. It tells you how to "count" the music. It looks like a fraction. The top number tells you the number of notes in the measure. The bottom number tells you the duration of the notes.

Different kinds of music have different rhythms or beats. Rock music usually has a regular 4/4 beat. A waltz and some country music are played in 3/4 time. Jigs are in 6/8 time, and so are some marches.

cymbal

cymbal

tom toms

hi-hat
cymbals

snare drum

floor
tom

A drummer uses hands and feet to play a drum set.

bass
drum

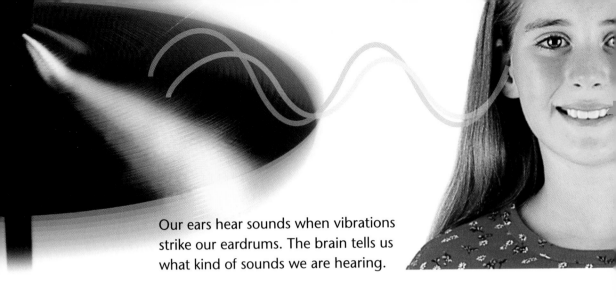

Our ears hear sounds when vibrations strike our eardrums. The brain tells us what kind of sounds we are hearing.

Pitch

Nature makes many sounds. The rustling of leaves is one example. All sounds have one thing in common. They are caused by **vibrations**.

A vibration is a rapid back-and-forth movement. Vibrations travel through the air to our ears. They travel in **waves**, like ripples made in water. Your ears detect these vibrations, and your brain interprets them as sound.

Visible Vibrations

Stretch a rubber band across a box. Pluck it. You will see the vibrations. If the rubber band is stretched tighter, it will vibrate faster. This makes a sound with a higher pitch.

The vibrations of a rubber band can easily be seen.

As instruments are struck, strummed, or blown into, different vibrations are created. Slow waves make low sounds. Fast waves make high sounds.

Vibrations can be felt as well as seen and heard. Lightly touch your lips and your throat with your fingertips; then hum. You will feel vibrations because the vocal cords in your throat are vibrating. As air passes over the vocal chords, sound is made. When the cords vibrate faster, they make a higher-pitched sound.

The vocal cords in your throat vibrate. You can feel the vibrations with your fingers.

The Talking Drum

The dundun is a talking drum. The Yoruba (YO roo ba) in Nigeria use the dundun to send messages. The player holds the drum under one arm. The drummer squeezes the strings, making the drumheads tighter or looser. This makes the pitch rise or fall, just like the human voice.

There are three ways to make the pitch of a vibrating object higher. You can make it thinner, shorter, or tighter. For a lower pitch, you must make the object thicker, longer, or looser.

When people sing, they make their vocal cords tighter or looser to make different pitches. Men's voices are usually lower than women's. That's because their vocal cords are longer.

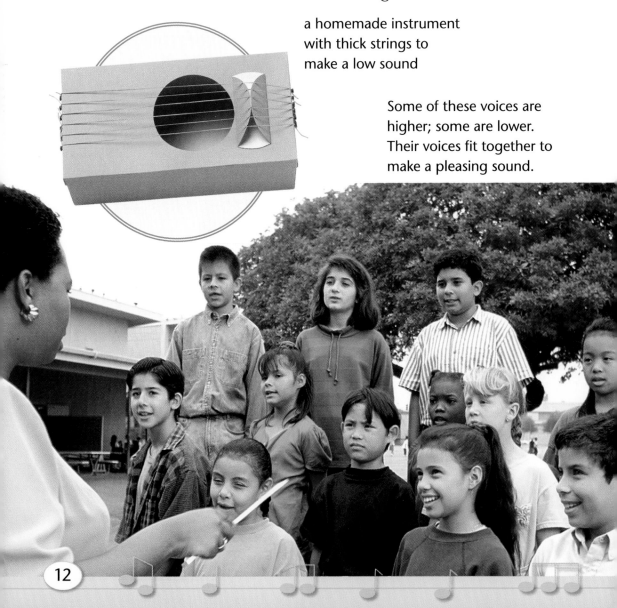

a homemade instrument with thick strings to make a low sound

Some of these voices are higher; some are lower. Their voices fit together to make a pleasing sound.

Scales

A **scale** is a row of notes in sequence. They go up or down in pitch. It's easy to see a scale on a piano or keyboard.

To play a major scale, start on middle C. Now move to the right, hitting eight white keys in all. The tone of each key is higher in pitch. The eighth note sounds like the middle C tone, one **octave** higher. It has twice as many vibrations per second than the first tone.

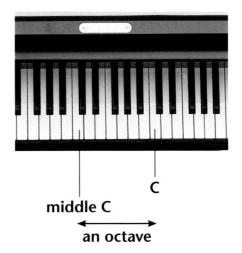

middle C

C

an octave

This is how a major scale starting on C is written.

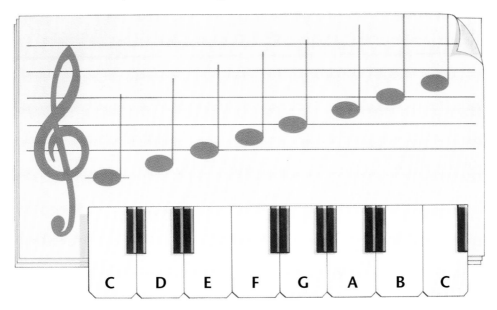

C D E F G A B C

The Black Keys

On a piano, the black keys are used to play sharps and flats. The sharp (shown by a # sign) of a note raises the pitch. The flat (shown by a ♭ sign) of a note lowers the pitch.

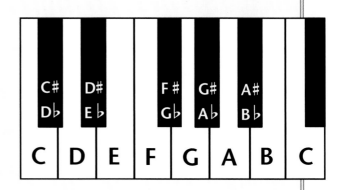

A major scale on a key other than C uses one or more black keys. This is because a major scale follows a pattern of notes: 2, 2, 1, 2, 2, 2, 1. That means moving two keys, then two more keys, then one key, and so on. When you hit the next white key after C, you move two notes, or tones, instead of one. You skip the black key.

musician Stevie Wonder at a keyboard

Major scales are used in many kinds of music around the world. Within the basic major scales are different kinds of scales. For example, a five-note scale is called **pentatonic** (*penta* = "five"; *tonic* = "tones"). It uses notes 1, 2, 3, 5, and 6 of the major scale.

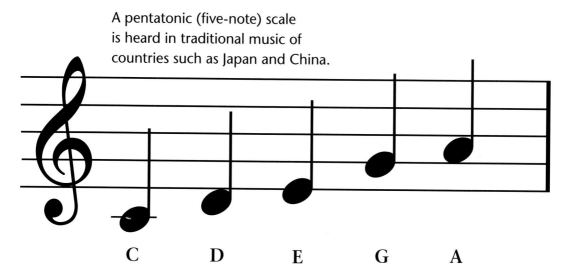

A pentatonic (five-note) scale is heard in traditional music of countries such as Japan and China.

C   D   E   G   A

The Minor Scale

In a minor scale, the third note is lowered by a tone. To many people, music played in a minor key sounds sad or mysterious. Think of music you hear when a TV show or movie is sad or scary. It is likely being played in a minor key.

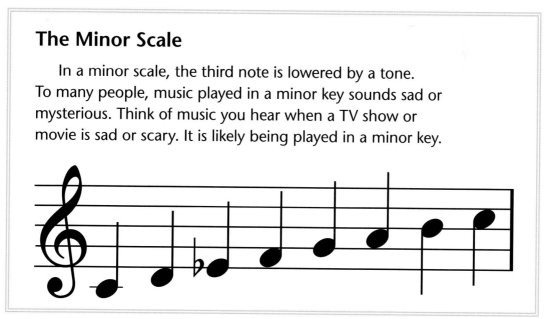

Instrument Families

There are many kinds of musical instruments. They can be divided into four different instrument families: string, woodwind, brass, and percussion instruments.

String Instruments

String instruments may have been discovered when people heard the "twang" sound from a hunting bow that had been plucked. The strings of these instruments vibrate when they are plucked, strummed, or played with a bow. Pressing a string makes the part that is vibrating shorter. This raises the number of vibrations and makes the pitch higher. The vibration changes can be described in fractions, such as halves and thirds.

The cello is played with a bow that is moved across the strings. The size of the cello's body creates low notes from the strings' vibrations.

The strings of a sitar from India are plucked.

Woodwind Instruments

Woodwind instruments began when people discovered that a sound can be made by blowing across an opening or making a reed vibrate.

The pitch of a woodwind instrument can be made higher or lower. The player does this by changing the length of the column of air. Holes in the side of the instrument are opened or closed to make these changes.

Native Americans made their flutes from hollow reeds or branches of trees.

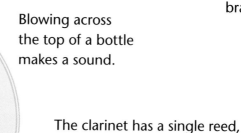

Blowing across the top of a bottle makes a sound.

The clarinet has a single reed, which vibrates against an opening in the mouthpiece.

The didgeridoo (DIG a re doo) is made of hollow tree limbs. The player creates a deep, resonating drone by blowing into one end, vibrating the lips, and humming at the same time.

Brass Instruments

In all brass instruments, the sound is produced in the same way. The player buzzes his or her lips against the metal mouthpiece. The buzzing vibrates the air in the pipes. When extra lengths of pipe are added, the vibrations have to travel farther. This makes the pitch lower. These added pitches are then used to play all the notes of the scale.

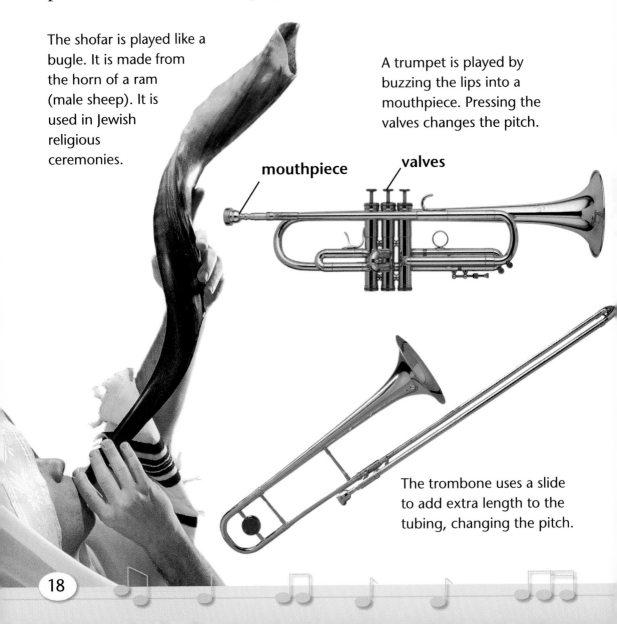

The shofar is played like a bugle. It is made from the horn of a ram (male sheep). It is used in Jewish religious ceremonies.

A trumpet is played by buzzing the lips into a mouthpiece. Pressing the valves changes the pitch.

mouthpiece

valves

The trombone uses a slide to add extra length to the tubing, changing the pitch.

Percussion Instruments

Any instrument that is struck to make a sound is a percussion instrument. These instruments include drums of all kinds, gongs and cymbals, chimes, and bars of wood. They may be struck with sticks, brushes, or hands.

Percussion instruments can also be shaken. The seeds or pellets inside a rattle strike the instrument and make it sound.

Gongs are an important part of South and East Asian music.

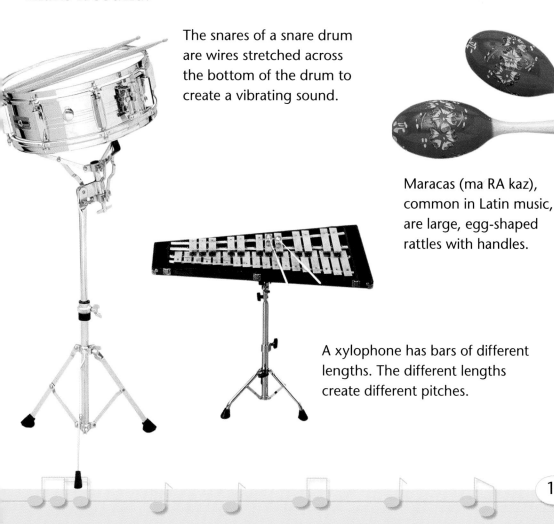

The snares of a snare drum are wires stretched across the bottom of the drum to create a vibrating sound.

Maracas (ma RA kaz), common in Latin music, are large, egg-shaped rattles with handles.

A xylophone has bars of different lengths. The different lengths create different pitches.

Music and the Mind

Can music make you smarter? Some people think it can. Some students score higher if they listen to classical music before taking a test.

The music of Mozart was used the first time this idea was tested. That's why the idea is called the Mozart **effect**. Clear, logical music like Mozart's seems to help people organize and focus their thoughts.

Some people think that children should hear classical music when they are young. They believe this will help their brains develop better.

Listening to classical music just before taking a test may help a person get a higher score.

Using music to heal both the mind and body is called **music therapy**. Musical therapists believe that classical music is best for healing. It helps the body, mind, and spirit work together in harmony through vibrations and energy. Music can also make people feel calmer. Feeling calmer helps people to heal and to focus less on pain and illness.

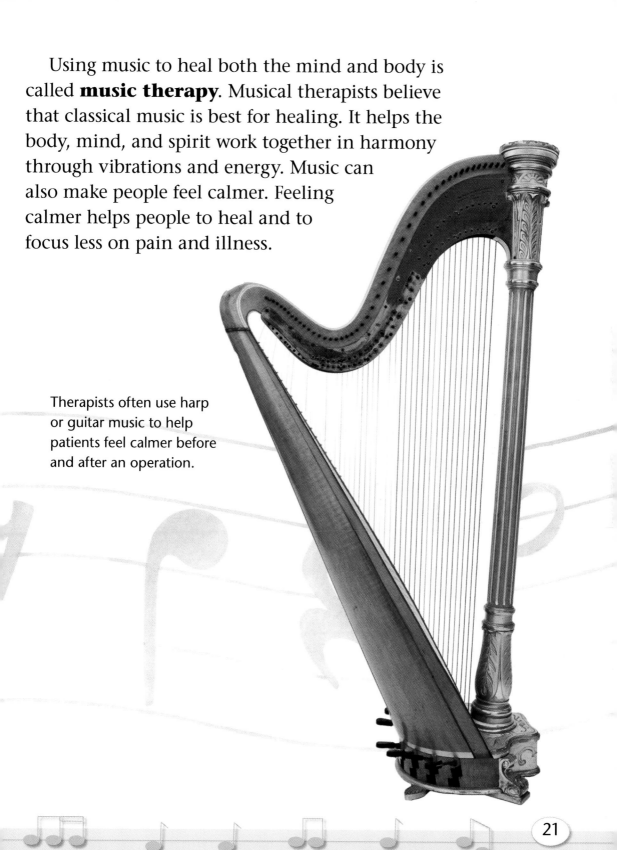

Therapists often use harp or guitar music to help patients feel calmer before and after an operation.

Music can cause an effect on the body in other ways, too. Fast music can make the heart beat faster. Slow music can help people relax. Pleasing music can make them feel better. Rhythmic music can make people want to dance.

Entertainment of all kinds uses music. Background music in movies or on TV helps to tell the story. It suggests fun, danger, suspense, or romance.

Music has always been a part of people's lives. Can you imagine a world without it?

Playing our own music is a way to be creative.

Glossary

duration	the length of a note
effect	something that is caused by another thing; a result
flat	a symbol (♭) showing that a note is lowered
music therapy	treatment that uses music to help people heal
octave	the eighth tone above or below a given tone, having twice or half as many vibrations per second
pentatonic	having five tones; a pentatonic scale has five tones
percussion	the striking of percussion instruments to produce tones
pitch	the high or low sound of a note
rhythm	the repetition of long and short sounds and silences in a particular pattern
scale	a sequence of tones going up or down in pitch. A major scale is an arrangement of eight notes using a 2, 2, 1, 2, 2, 2, 1 pattern of keys. A minor scale has the third note lowered (flatted).
sharp	a symbol (#) showing that a note is raised
staff	a set of five horizontal lines on which music is written
time signature	a sign that shows the number and type of notes in a measure. The top number tells the number of notes in the measure; the bottom number tells the duration of the notes. Also called meter signature
tone	the sound a note tells the player to make
vibrations	rapid, rhythmic movements back and forth
waves	moving ridges or swells that carry light, heat, water, or sound

Index